20TH CENTURY *music*

80s & 90s

DIFFERENT PATHS

Please visit our web site at: www.garethstevens.com
For a free color catalog describing Gareth Stevens Publishing's list of high-quality books
and multimedia programs, call 1-800-542-2595 or fax your request to (414) 332-3567.

Library of Congress Cataloging-in-Publication Data

Hayes, Malcolm.
    80s & 90s: different paths / by Malcolm Hayes.
       p. cm. — (20th century music)
    Includes bibliographical references and index.
    Summary: Discusses the influence of people and events worldwide in the late twentieth
century which led to crossover between musical genres, stadium rock fund-raisers, hip-hop,
rap, and the rise of world music.
    ISBN 0-8368-3036-9 (lib. bdg.)
    1. Music—20th century—History and criticism—Juvenile literature. [1. Music—20th
century—History and criticism.] I. Title: 80s and 90s. II. Title. III. 20th century music.
ML3928.H365   2002
780'.9'04—dc21   2001054222

This North American edition first published in 2002 by
Gareth Stevens Publishing
A World Almanac Education Group Company
330 West Olive Street, Suite 100
Milwaukee, WI 53212 USA

Original edition © 2001 by David West Children's Books. First published in Great Britain
in 2001 by Heinemann Library, Halley Court, Jordan Hill, Oxford OX2 8EJ, a division of Reed
Educational and Professional Publishing Limited. This U.S. edition © 2002 by Gareth Stevens, Inc.
Additional end matter © 2002 by Gareth Stevens, Inc.

Designer: Rob Shone
Editor: James Pickering
Picture Research: Carrie Haines

Gareth Stevens Editor: Alan Wachtel

Photo Credits:
Abbreviations: (t) top, (m) middle, (b) bottom, (l) left, (r) right

Sally Chappell/The Art Archive/Victoria and Albert Museum: page 10(mr).
Flpo Musto/LFI-IM/London Features Int. Ltd.: page 16(bl).
Frank Forcino/LFI-UFF/London Features Int. Ltd.: page 5(tl).
The Kobal Collection: page 12(tr).
Lebrecht Collection: pages 26(br); 29(m) (Victor Bazlenov); 29(tr) (David Farrell); 4(b), 6(l), 6-7(t),
    7(m), 8(br), 9(bl), 11(r), 25(tr), 26(t, bl) (Betty Freeman); 28(r) (Alexandra Kremer); 13(t) (Laurie
    Lewis); 24(r), 28(bl) (Nigel Luckhurst); 10(bl) (Suzie Maecler); 6(r), 8-9(t) (Alastair Muir); 25(bl),
    27(m) (Richard H. Smith); 29(bl) (Sally Whyte).
Robert Lowell/Hulton Getty: page 9(mr).
Performing Art Library: page 13(m, b).
Redferns: cover (m) (AA/DR 9019); cover (br), page 27(tr) (Malcolm Crowther); pages 18(l) (Richie
    Aaron); 3, 15(tl) (Paul Bergen); 15(br) (Sue Cunningham); 16(br) (Kieran Doherty); 20-21(t) (Tim
    Hall); 4(t), 19(t), 22(l) (Mick Hutson); 15(ml), 17(tr) (Bob King); 22(b) (J. Krebbs); 21(m) (Chi
    Modu); 21(tr) (Albert Ortega); 5(tr) (Roberta Parkin); 12(br), 14(m), 17(tl), 22-23(t), 23(both),
    (David Redfern); 5(br), 14(bl), 17(m), 19(m, b), 20(b) (Ebet Roberts); 24(l) (Nicky J. Simms);
    16(tr) (Peter Still); 20(t) (Jon Super).
Rex Features: pages 18(tr); 27(b) (Brooker).
Mark Taylor: page 8(l).

Printed in the United States of America

1 2 3 4 5 6 7 8 9 06 05 04 03 02

20TH CENTURY music
80s & 90s
DIFFERENT PATHS

Malcolm Hayes

Gareth Stevens Publishing
A WORLD ALMANAC EDUCATION GROUP COMPANY

CONTENTS

Illness took its toll on the career of Miles Davis (1926–1991), but in the early 1980s, he re-established himself as one of jazz's greatest trumpeters.

George Benjamin (b. 1960) studied with Olivier Messiaen in Paris and quickly became famous with his orchestral work Ringed by the Flat Horizon *(1980).*

A COMFORTABLE AGE

After appearing on Paul Simon's album Graceland *(1986), the South African Zulu choir Ladysmith Black Mambazo became a force in world music.*

Kurt Cobain (1967–1994) led Nirvana to huge success with the albums Nevermind *(1991) and* In Utero *(1993).*

With his album Born in the USA *(1984), Bruce Springsteen (b. 1949) became one of the kings of stadium rock.*

The closing decades of the 20th century were a time of strange contradictions. By the mid-1990s, the communist governments of eastern Europe and the Soviet Union had fallen and were replaced by often troubled attempts at Western-style democracy. Meanwhile, the West was in an era of political stability and economic prosperity. The times were steadier, but they were also less dramatic.

Compared to the liberated 1960s and the turbulent and excessive 1970s, the music of the 20th century's last two decades was far less radical. In classical music, rock, and jazz, styles and techniques, and the opportunities for mixing them, were more varied than ever. When artists tried to blend styles, however, blandness was often the result. So, different musical styles became pigeonholed and more separate than before. Nonetheless, truly strong individual talents grew and flourished as they always have. The end of the century was a time of creative individualism, and with the arrival of digital technology and the huge growth of specialized radio stations, music was everywhere.

MINIMALISM AND OPERA

With its emphasis on listener-friendly, conventional harmony and easy-to-follow musical patterns, minimalism had broad appeal in the new age of musical accessibility, while modernism did not. The best minimalist composers, however, produced works that soared far above predictable mediocrity.

John Adams's complex harmonic style is rooted in the European symphonic tradition of the 19th and early 20th centuries, especially the works of Jean Sibelius.

A REMARKABLE FIRST OPERA

American composer John Adams (*b.* 1947) made his international breakthrough with *Harmonium* (1980), a piece for chorus and orchestra. The music's appealing sound, range of invention, and sheer drama all indicated the arrival of a composer with major potential. Adams followed this work with his first opera, *Nixon in China* (1985–1987), which was first staged at the Houston Opera in 1987. Its success showed that minimalism could have the inventive range to make a large-scale opera work impressively on the stage, in both musical and dramatic terms.

Nixon (at bottom of steps) *arriving in China in a scene from Adams's opera*

REALISTIC OPERA

Nixon in China portrays the events of Richard Nixon's visit, the first by an American president, to the communist People's Republic of China in 1972. This opera brilliantly mixes a documentary approach with musical imagination and dramatic effectiveness that clearly connects to operatic tradition. It's style might be described as "opera as reporting!"

Steve Reich (center, rear) rehearses with his ensemble. The interplay between Reich's favorite lineup of percussion instruments is much harder to perform than it sounds, so each concert requires a lot of practice.

POLITICAL CONFLICT

The Death of Klinghoffer (1991), John Adams's next opera, was fiercely controversial. It portrayed the hijacking of the Mediterranean cruise ship *Achille Lauro,* including the murder of an elderly Jewish passenger named Klinghoffer, by a group of Palestinian terrorists. It also portrayed the wider political troubles in the Middle East that were behind this event. Adams's latest large-scale work is *El Niño* (1999–2000), an oratorio about the Christmas nativity story, which uses texts in English, Latin, and Spanish.

GLASS AND REICH

Steve Reich (*b.* 1936) produced the large-scale works *Tehillim* (1981) and *The Desert Music* (1983), for chorus and orchestra. Philip Glass (*b.* 1937) achieved wide success with his operas *Satyagraha* (1980), about the early days of the nonviolent resistance movement started by Mahatma Gandhi, and *Akhnaten* (1984), about an Egyptian pharaoh. Glass also composed the score for the film *Koyaanisqatsi* (1982).

The oddly spelled CIVIL warS *was a huge project by theater director Robert Wilson that involved several composers. Philip Glass (above) completed* Act V (Rome Section) *in 1983. Doris Lessing's science fiction story was the basis for Glass's opera* The Making of the Representative for Planet 8 *(1988).*

In Akhnaten, *Glass suggests the story's distant time and place by creating a strange sound. His music uses no violins, so the orchestral coloring is much darker than usual.*

MODERNISM LIVES!

As audiences for classical music became larger and wealthier, they mostly wanted, or believed they wanted, music that was easier to listen to. Challenging modern classical music, however, was far from dead, as the works of its leading composers showed magnificently.

BIRTWISTLE'S ROOTS

Although Birtwistle is a world-famous composer, he remains in touch with his roots. The hero in *The Mask of Orpheus* enters the underworld by crossing a bridge with seventeen arches, much like the railroad viaduct near the town of Accrington, England, where Birtwistle was born.

Accrington Viaduct inspired one of the great scenes of modern opera.

ORPHEUS SINGS ON AN EPIC SCALE

English composer Harrison Birtwistle (*b.* 1934) worked on his massive three-act opera, *The Mask of Orpheus*, for ten years before completing it in 1983. The opera is about the singer of ancient Greek legend who visits the underworld to try to bring his dead bride, Euridice, back to life. Birtwistle's opera presents the story of Orpheus in a ritualistic, multilayered way, so that, in places, different versions of the legend are presented on stage at the same time. The result is a musical drama of immense power.

Like Birtwistle (right), Austrian-born pianist Alfred Brendel (b. 1931), who plays mostly traditional works, is deeply interested in modern music.

8

MORE OPERAS

Birtwistle's next opera was *Gawain* (1991). This work takes a similar, multilayered approach to the story of Sir Gawain, who, in Celtic legend, is one of the knights of King Arthur's Round Table. The opera tells of Gawain's duel with Arthur's enemy, the sinister Green Knight. Birtwistle's most recent opera is *The Last Supper* (2000), based on the biblical story of Jesus and his disciples, viewed from the perspective of the turbulent and war torn 20th century.

EVER THE EXPLORER

Throughout his career, American Elliott Carter (*b.* 1908) has composed works full of complex ideas, such as his large-scale, three-movement *Symphonia* (1993–1996). His song cycle *In Sleep, in Thunder* (1981) set to music words by American poet Robert Lowell. At age 90, Carter completed his first opera, *What Next?* It was first performed in Berlin in 1999.

9

The Green Knight's head continues to sing after being cut off by Sir Gawain.

The words of Robert Lowell, an important 20th-century American poet, also inspired the cantata Phaedra *by Benjamin Britten.*

The success of Elliott Carter's (left) *later music owes much to the conducting skill of Oliver Knussen (b. 1952)* (right), *whose own works include the children's operas* Where the Wild Things Are *(1983) and* Higglety Pigglety Pop! *(1985).*

SOUNDS OF MUSIC

Modern classical music in France was dominated by two extremely influential, and distinctly different, master composers, Olivier Messiaen and Pierre Boulez. The musical history of the second half of the 20th century would have been very different without them.

THE SAINT AND THE WINGED SINGERS

Olivier Messiaen (1908–1992) worked on his only opera, *Saint François d'Assise*, between 1975 and 1983, when it was first staged at the Paris Opera. It tells the story of the life and death of St. Francis of Assisi, a medieval Italian saint, in a series of eight, frescolike scenes. Some of the scenes are very long. For instance, St. Francis's sermon to the birds lasts over an hour. It is the grandest and most elaborate example of Messiaen's technique of setting birdsong into musical terms.

SACRED SPIRIT

Messiaen described his Catholic faith as "the one aspect of my life that I will not regret at the hour of my death." Until old age prevented it, he played the organ, as he had since the 1930s, at Mass every Sunday in the Church of Sainte-Trinité in Paris. Music, for Messiaen, was a manifestation of God's presence on Earth.

The Transfiguration *by English artist William Blake (1757–1827), who, like Messiaen, was inspired by religious themes*

In the 1980s, Messiaen's music was often performed in England, where he worked with conductor John Carewe (b. 1933) (left).

MESSIAEN'S LAST THOUGHTS

Messiaen's interest in birdsong was both musical and symbolic. For him, each bird represented a soul resurrected from the dead by Christ's self-sacrifice, and its song expressed that soul's eternal joy. Birdsong is featured in Messiaen's largest organ work, *Livre du Saint Sacrement,* or *Book of the Holy Sacrament,* (1984–1986). His last major creation was *Eclairs sur l'au-delà,* or *Rays on the Beyond,* (1989–1992), which has ten orchestral movements.

Equipment that used to be very bulky is now easily portable. Today, computers powerful enough to generate or transform sounds can be set up in spaces ranging in size from a small home studio to a huge concert hall.

COMPOSING WITH COMPUTERS

Pierre Boulez (*b.* 1925) divides his time between his conducting career and his work as director of the Institut de Recherche et Coordination Acoustique/ Musique (IRCAM), a center, located in Paris, for research into computer-generated musical sound. Boulez has produced two ongoing "works in progress" that use both conventional instruments and computers: *Explosante-fixe,* or *Exploding-stationary,* (started in 1971) and *Répons,* or *Response(s),* (started in 1981). Boulez has also reworked his cantata *Le Visage Nuptial,* or *The Nuptial Countenance,* (1946). He completed the revision in 1989.

Boulez is committed to exploring the musical possibilities opened up by the use of computer-generated and computer-manipulated sound.

Messiaen could transcribe even the fastest and highest-pitched birdsong by slowing it down and lowering it and also by harmonizing it.

MUSICALS

Musical theater had long been an American art form. In the 1980s and 1990s, however, one of the most successful composers of musicals was from England — but his music swept the world.

MEGASTAR OF THE MUSICAL STAGE

Andrew Lloyd Webber (*b.* 1948) is the son of composer William Lloyd Webber (1914–1982) and the brother of cellist Julian Lloyd Webber (*b.* 1951). His earlier successful musicals included *Joseph and the Amazing Technicolor Dreamcoat* (1968, expanded in 1972), *Jesus Christ Superstar* (1971), and *Evita* (1978). Then came *Cats* (1981), which is based on poems by T. S. Eliot; *Starlight Express* (1984); and *The Phantom of the Opera* (1986). Late in 2001, *The Phantom of the Opera* was still playing at Broadway theaters.

A VERSATILE GIFT

Lloyd Webber's talent is being able to work in different styles to suit each project while keeping his own unmistakable musical signature. *Cats* mixes songs, spoken dialogue, and dance in the classic way; *Starlight Express* is more of a rock musical; and *The Phantom of the Opera* has the long passages of an opera. Other Lloyd Webber hits include *Aspects of Love* (1989) and *Sunset Boulevard* (1993).

LATIN AMERICAN HEROINE

Evita was Andrew Lloyd Webber's final work with lyricist Tim Rice. This musical is based on the life of Evita Duarte, wife of populist Argentinian president Juan Perón. In 1996, Warner Brothers released a movie version, starring Madonna in the title role. For the film, Rice and Lloyd Webber wrote an additional song, "You Must Love Me."

Madonna in the role of Evita

Andrew Lloyd Webber rarely performs live and prefers to stay out of the spotlight. His newest musical, with lyrics by Ben Elton, is The Beautiful Game *(2000). It is about soccer-loving teenagers in the 1960s.*

Lyricist and composer Stephen Sondheim is the king of the Broadway musical.

PUSH BAR

AN AMERICAN MASTER

Stephen Sondheim (*b.* 1930) came to fame in 1957 as the brilliant lyricist of Leonard Bernstein's *West Side Story*. Sondheim's musicals often explore unusual subjects in innovative ways. *Sunday in the Park with George* (1984), set in Paris, was inspired by a painting by French artist Georges Seurat that hangs in the Art Institute of Chicago. *Into the Woods* (1991) is based on Grimm Brothers' fairy tales. *Passion* (1994) is set in 1860s Italy.

Based on Victor Hugo's novel about conditions in France after the French Revolution, Les Misérables opened on Broadway in 1987 and is still running.

In Sondheim's Into the Woods, familiar fairy-tale characters, such as Little Red Riding Hood, Jack the Giant-Killer, and Cinderella, encounter nightmare situations that are unfamiliar from their stories, but, in the end, optimism and happiness are restored.

EMBRACING THE WORLD

After the excesses of the 1970s, rock needed to explore new musical territory. Much the way people in the increasingly affluent 1980s were traveling more widely than ever before, popular music began to do the same.

Hugh Masekela was cofounder of the Jazz Epistles, the first black South African band to record a jazz album.

14

Paul Simon (center, in white shirt) *performs songs from* Graceland *with Ladysmith Black Mambazo. Simon was accused of exploiting African musicians, but* Graceland *did much to increase the global success of world music.*

PAUL SIMON MAKES NEW FRIENDS

After successes both with Art Garfunkel (*b.* 1941) and as a solo artist, Paul Simon (*b.* 1941) found a new direction with *Graceland* (1986). This album started with tapes he made of black South African musicians, which he worked on further in New York to turn the music into pop songs. The result was a kind of "world music" that brought unfamiliar African sounds to Western ears. Simon followed *Graceland* with *The Rhythm of the Saints* (1990), which features Brazilian drumming.

LATE, BUT SWEET, SUCCESS

In 1996, American musician Ry Cooder brought together some legends of Cuban folk and jazz music to record the *Buena Vista Social Club*. This album caught the world-music mood of the 1990s and was a great success for the elderly musicians. German filmmaker Wim Wenders made a documentary about the group and filmed their 1998 sellout concert at New York's Carnegie Hall.

Cuban masters with guitarist Ry Cooder (right)

OUT OF AFRICA

The Zulu group Ladysmith Black Mambazo was among those performing on *Graceland*. The group went on to world fame with albums such as *Shaka Zulu* (1987), produced by Paul Simon, and *The Star and the Wise Man* (1998), with Simon and country singer Dolly Parton (*b.* 1946). South Africa's great trumpet and flugelhorn player Hugh Masekela (*b.* 1939) also toured with Simon and has made many albums in his own African jazz style.

In 1989, David Byrne (pictured here on a visit to Moscow) left the Talking Heads and concentrated on albums influenced by world music, including Uh-Oh *(1992) and* Feelings *(1997).*

GOING SOLO

In 1980, David Byrne (*b.* 1952) took a break from his group Talking Heads to work with Brian Eno (*b.* 1948) on *My Life in the Bush of Ghosts*. This album featured Egyptian singers and Islamic chant. On his *Rei Momo* (1989), Byrne is backed by Brazilian musicians. Sting (*b.* Gordon Sumner, 1951), formerly of The Police, made his first solo album, *The Dream of the Blue Turtles*, a jazz-rock crossover, in 1985. Sting also helped start the Rainforest Foundation to help fight the ecological threat to the Brazilian Indian population.

For a while, Sting was more involved with ecological work than with music. In 1989, he took Brazilian Indian Chief Raoni on a worldwide publicity tour.

ROCK BANDS

Spectacularly successful bands on both sides of the Atlantic drew their fans to huge stadium concerts. The group that sold the most tickets was also the one that had been around the longest.

Geldof (left) with U2's lead singer, Bono, at Live Aid

THE STONES KEEP ON ROLLING

Since their impressive rock 'n' roll successes of the 1960s, the Rolling Stones never lost their audience, especially in the United States. In 1981, the Stones broke new ground by planning and organizing the first tour that took 1970s-style stadium rock around the world, complete with new songs, massive amplification, and spectacular light shows. After *Tattoo You* (1981) came more albums, including *Bridges to Babylon* (1997), and tours every few years, with Mick Jagger (*b.* 1943) and Keith Richards (*b.* 1943) leading the show.

16

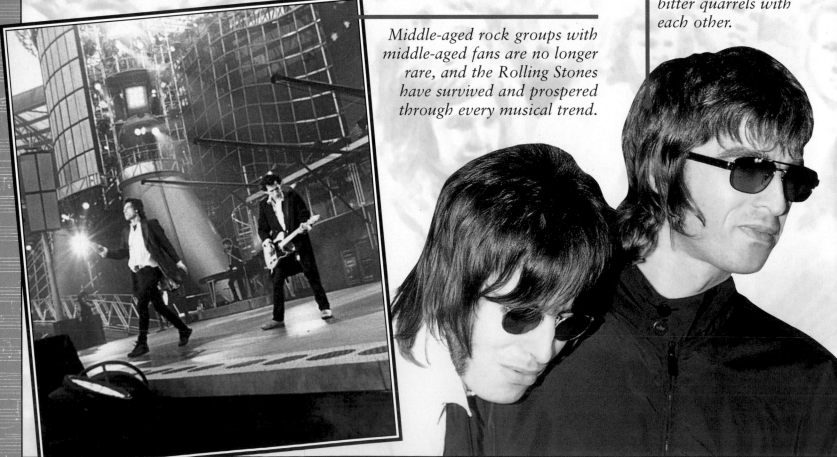

Middle-aged rock groups with middle-aged fans are no longer rare, and the Rolling Stones have survived and prospered through every musical trend.

The Gallagher brothers of the group Oasis, singer Liam (left) and songwriter/ guitarist Noel, are notorious for their bitter quarrels with each other.

HELPING THE HUNGRY

Held in 1985 at London's Wembley Stadium and Philadelphia's JFK Stadium, the Live Aid concert was organized by Bob Geldof (*b.* 1954) of the Boomtown Rats to raise money for victims of famine in Africa. Many of rock music's leading artists, including U2, Queen, and Mick Jagger, performed for free. Classic rock bands Led Zeppelin and The Who reformed for the event.

Live Aid was a worldwide television event, during which Geldof asked the billions who were watching for donations.

Fronted by Michael Stipe (b. 1960) R.E.M. offset the excesses of stadium rock with their exceptional songwriting.

Live Aid inspired Queen's song "One Vision." The group, formed in 1971, disbanded when singer Freddie Mercury (right) died in 1991.

1990s BRITPOP

The success of Oasis in the 1990s showed that rock was in the mood for something similar to 1960s pop, but with a sharper 1990s edge. Formed in Manchester in 1993 by the Gallagher brothers, Liam (*b.* 1972), and Noel (*b.* 1967), the group hurtled to world fame with the albums *Definitely Maybe* (1994) and (*What's the Story*) *Morning Glory?* (1995). Radiohead, formed at a school in Oxford in 1988, offered a melancholy contrast with *Pablo Honey* (1993), *The Bends* (1995), and *OK Computer* (1997).

SHORT NAMES AND BIG AIMS

Ireland's U2 and its lead singer Bono (*b.* Paul Hewson, 1960) had already made their names with the ambitious and politically charged albums *War* (1983) and *The Unforgettable Fire* (1984), when they dazzled the world with *The Joshua Tree* (1987). America's pacesetter was R.E.M., who used raging electric tracks and gentle acoustic sounds on albums such as *Lifes Rich Pageant* (1986), *Out of Time* (1991), *Monster* (1994), and *Up* (1998).

POP SUPERSTARS

With its range of singers and songwriters, pop music was as varied as ever, and record companies and radio stations increasingly marketed the work of musical performers to particular groups of listeners. This approach was far from the *Graceland* spirit of bringing different musical worlds together.

John Lennon at his New York apartment

TWO WOMEN

The most successful female pop artist ever, Madonna (*b.* Madonna Ciccone, 1958) found stardom with *Like a Virgin* (1984). Her later albums, including *Like a Prayer* (1989), *Something to Remember* (1995), and *Ray of Light* (1998), show both her songwriting talent and her flair for reinventing her image. Less productive but with a passionate following in Britain, Kate Bush (*b.* 1958) recorded the adventurous albums *Hounds of Love* (1985), *The Sensual World* (1989), and *The Red Shoes* (1993).

Madonna's film appearances have not matched her success as a singer, but the movie Desperately Seeking Susan *(1984) features one of her best songs, "Into the Groove." She also appeared in the film version of Andrew Lloyd Webber's musical* Evita.

18

A LIFE CUT SHORT

The up-and-down, post-Beatles career of John Lennon (1940–1980) included some fine material on *John Lennon and the Plastic Ono Band* (1971) and *Imagine* (1971). In late 1980, Lennon emerged after a five-year break to record *Double Fantasy*. He was working on a new album, *Milk and Honey* (1984), when he was murdered by a crazed fan outside his New York home.

THREE MEGASTARS

Michael Jackson (*b*. 1958), one of the original Jackson Five, peaked in 1982 with the megahit album *Thriller*. The album sold 40 million copies, which was a world record for nearly 20 years. Prince (*b*. Prince Rogers Nelson, 1958) also emerged as a major musical talent, drawing together rock, rhythm and blues, and funk. *Purple Rain* (1984) is one of his biggest hit albums. Among his other albums are *Parade* (1986) and *Diamonds and Pearls* (1992). After making *Listen Without Prejudice, Vol. 1* (1990), George Michael (*b*. Georgios Panayiotou, 1963) sued his his record company, Sony, for inadequately promoting his music.

AMERICAN ROOTS

Bruce Springsteen (*b*. 1949) achieved immortality with his storming live performances and his working-class image reflected in his album *Born in the USA* (1984). Garth Brooks (*b*. 1962) became the reigning king of pop country and western music. Brooks's wide commercial appeal contrasts with newly revived, folk-rooted bluegrass music.

In 1993, Prince announced that this unpronounceable icon was his new name. Most fans just called him "The Artist Formerly Known As Prince."

In spite of country music's limited appeal outside America, Garth Brooks was probably the world's biggest selling pop country recording artist of the 1990s.

Michael Jackson made elaborate music videos to help promote his songs. The dancing and special effects on the Thriller *video set new standards for music videos.*

HOUSE, HIP-HOP, AND RAP

Unlike classical music's emphasis on melody and harmony, much popular music throughout the 20th century focused on rhythm. House, hip-hop, and rap were the essence of music made for dancing in the late 20th century.

The Prodigy is one of the few British bands in recent years to top record charts in America.

Licensed to Ill (1986) and Check Your Head *(1992) were two of New York's Beastie Boys best-selling albums.*

DANCE TILL YOU DROP

House music was named after the Warehouse, the Chicago club where this high-energy style was first played. In 1987, Steve "Silk" Hurley (*b.* 1962) came up with "Jack Your Body," house music's first No. 1 hit single. By the early 1990s, house and other types of "dance music" had swept England. The Prodigy starred with their albums *Experience* (1992) and *Music for The Jilted Generation* (1995) and with the hit single "Firestarter" (1996).

"MADCHESTER"

Manchester England's Hacienda Club, which opened in 1982, quickly became a huge dance music attraction. While New Order influenced the rougher mood of 1990s dance music with the single "Blue Monday" and their album *Power, Corruption, and Lies* (both 1983), the nonstop, bouncing rhythm of bands such as the Happy Mondays and the Stone Roses defined the late 1980s "Manchester sound."

New Order evolved from the punk band Joy Division.

Ice-T seems proud of having been shot twice during an armed robbery. His albums include Rhyme Pays *(1987) and* Original Gangster *(1991).*

RAP'S ROOTS

Hip-hop started in the black communities of New York. Disc jockeys (DJs) started switching suddenly between records playing on different turntables and rhythmically scratching the records with the needle while a "rapper" improvised spoken dialogue over the music's beat. Hip-hop soon became an expression of rebellious urban youth, personified by groups such as Public Enemy, Run DMC, and the Beastie Boys. Rapper Will Smith (*b.* 1968) conveyed a happier attitude with *He's the DJ, I'm the Rapper* (1988) and *Big Willie Style* (1997).

Will Smith is both a rapper and an actor. He is one of the few major rap artists who avoid using foul language. Smith has had starring roles in many films, including Men in Black *(1997).*

THE DARK SIDE OF RAP

Gangsta rap had gangland links, and violent feuds between artists, managers, and record labels became regular occurrences. Rap superstars Tupac Shakur (1971–1996) and Notorious B.I.G. (Christopher Wallace, 1972–1997) were killed in these conflicts. In the late 1980s, the influential group Public Enemy supported rap's Stop the Violence movement. Surviving gangsta rappers include Ice Cube (*b.* O'Shea Jackson, 1969), Dr. Dre (*b.* Andre Young, 1965), Ice-T (*b.* Tracy Morrow, 1959); and Puff Daddy (*b.* Sean Combs, 1970).

MODERN JAZZ MASTERS

In the 1980s and 1990s, jazz continued to expand, learning from world music and making greater use of high-tech instruments. Some jazz artists of the time were also fine classical musicians.

ULTIMATE MASTERY

The fantastically gifted pianist Keith Jarrett (*b*. 1945) gave a remarkable series of concerts, often playing alone, but sometimes in a jazz trio with bass and drums. Many of the concerts, including his legendary solo improvisations in Vienna, Austria (1991), and Milan, Italy (1995), were recorded on the ECM record label, which releases many different kinds of modern music.

With *Spirits* (1985), featuring Pakistani flute and ethnic chanting, Jarrett connected jazz with world music. Also a classical pianist, Jarrett made an outstanding recording of Mozart's Piano Concertos with the Stuttgart Chamber Orchestra in 1996.

Keith Jarrett became ill with chronic fatigue syndrome in the late 1990s and, for a time, was too sick to perform. He has since returned to recording and performing.

In 1980, after several years of ill health, Miles Davis returned to the world of jazz and made several albums, including The Man with the Horn *(1981) and* Decoy *(1983), before he died in 1991.*

22

THE MARSALIS BROTHERS

Not only did classically-trained trumpeter Wynton Marsalis (*b.* 1961) play on jazz albums, such as *Blue Interlude* (1991), with his own seven-piece band, but he also played on the 1984 recording of Leonard Bernstein's *West Side Story*. His brother, saxophonist Branford Marsalis (*b.* 1960), tackled a fusion of jazz and hip-hop on *Buckshot LeFonque* (1994). Branford also played on Sting's first two solo albums and with Herbie Hancock.

The Marsalis brothers helped keep jazz alive in the 1980s and 1990s.

KINGS OF THE KEYBOARDS

Although Herbie Hancock (*b.* 1940) is a classically-trained pianist, he became famous as an imaginative and experimental jazz-fusion composer and performer. *Future Shock* (1983), emphasizes the sound of electronic keyboards and contains the hit song "Rockit." *Gershwin's World* (1998) is a tribute to George Gershwin's hundredth birthday. Hancock also worked and toured with fellow-pianist Chick Corea (*b.* 1941), who recorded the *Mozart Sessions* (1996) and later composed his own Piano Concerto (1999).

23

Among Hancock's important albums were Quartet *(1981),* Hot and Heavy *(1984), and* A Tribute to Miles *(1992).*

TALENT TWICE OVER

The Brecker Brothers, trumpeter Randy (*b.* 1945) and saxophonist Michael (*b.* 1949), led a group together until 1982, when they separated to pursue individual musical careers. In 1992, they reunited for *Return of the Brecker Brothers*. Michael is known as a pioneer of the EWI, or Electronic Wind Instrument, a kind of extended saxophone with a huge, nine-octave range. Michael has also toured with Paul Simon.

Randy Brecker (right) studied classical trumpet and then played with Art Blakey and Stevie Wonder among others. Michael played saxophone in the band Steps Ahead before launching his own group.

ITALY AND GERMANY

The best modern classical music produced in Italy and Germany during the 1980s and 1990s was written by a few talented composers. These artists were able to maintain their powers of creative self-renewal over a very long time.

THE REVOLUTION CONTINUES

Hans Werner Henze remained true to the left-wing political stance he held earlier in his life. His opera *The English Cat* (1983) is a satire of capitalist and middle-class society in Victorian England, with the characters portrayed as cats. Henze's Ninth Symphony (1997), which uses voices and orchestra in a way that is similar to Beethoven's Ninth Symphony, is a fierce condemnation of Germany's Nazi past.

Hans Werner Henze (b. 1926)

Stockhausen's music became more popular among classical music fans in the 1990s. A major retrospective of his work was performed at the 1995 Salzburg Easter Festival.

A NEW SPIN ON THE STRING QUARTET

The passing of time did not mellow the avant-garde tendencies of Germany's Karlheinz Stockhausen (*b.* 1928). In 1977, he started work on *Licht*, or *Light*, a huge cycle of seven operas, one named after each day of the week. The cycle is almost complete. Only *Sonntag aus Licht*, or *Sunday from Light*, remains to be written. One of the scenes from *Mittwoch aus Licht*, or *Wednesday from Light*, (1992–1998) is the already legendary *Helicopter String Quartet* (1993), in which the four members of a string quartet each play their parts in separate, flying helicopters, linked with each other by closed-circuit television.

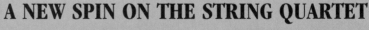

QUIET SOUNDS

In the mid-1970s, Italy's Luigi Nono (1924–1990) abandoned the left-wing political content of his earlier music and concentrated on composing very spare works in which he seemed to be searching for the quietest essence of musical sound. The largest of these works is *Prometeo*, or *Prometheus*, (1984). Others are *Fragmente-Stille — an Diotima*, or *Fragments-Silence — to Diotima*, (1980), dedicated to Nono's daughter; and *No hay caminos, hay que caminar...*, or *There are no pathways, only the traveling itself...*, (1987), for seven instrumental groups.

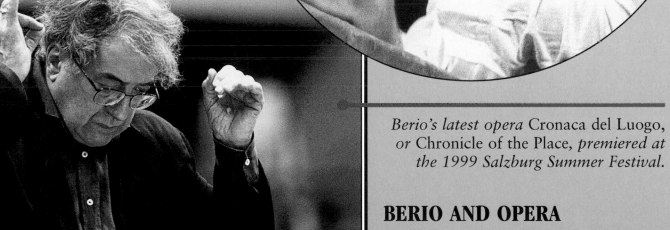

25

BERIO AND OPERA

In the last decades of the century, Luciano Berio (*b.* 1925) continued to produce works that showed his mastery of vocal and instrumental sound. Berio collaborated with Italian novelist Italo Calvino on two operas, *La Vera Storia*, or *The True Story*, (1982) and *Un Re in Ascolto*, or *A King Listens*, (1984).

ENGLAND AND SCOTLAND

In England, the best classical music of the time was created by maverick composers whose work had little in common with that of their counterparts on the European continent. Scotland also produced two major composers.

TIPPETT, BENJAMIN, AND TURNAGE

Among the late works of English composer Michael Tippett (1905–1998) were the non-religious oratorio *The Mask of Time* (1982) and his fifth opera, *New Year* (1991). Also on the scene during this time were two gifted young newcomers. George Benjamin (*b.* 1960), who was a student of Messiaen, caused a stir with *Ringed by the Flat Horizon* (1980) and *Antara* (1987), written for a chamber group playing with recorded and computer-enhanced panpipes. Mark-Anthony Turnage (*b.* 1960) attracted attention with the operas *Greek* (1988) and *The Silver Tassie* (1997–1999).

Turnage's music has roots in both the mood and techniques of jazz. Your Rockaby (1993) is a concerto for soprano saxophone and orchestra.

George Benjamin is an expert pianist and conducts both his own and others' music.

Tippett's late works included his Triple Concerto (1980), for violin, viola, cello, and orchestra, and a Fifth String Quartet (1991).

ORTHODOX RELIGION, UNORTHODOX MUSIC

John Tavener (*b.* 1944) composed music based on the ancient chants of the Eastern Orthodox, or Byzantine, Church. *The Protecting Veil* (1989), for cello and strings, achieved wide success. Tavener's largest musical statements included the monumental *Apocalypse* (1995) and *Fall and Resurrection* (1999), both for soloists, chorus, and orchestra.

TWO SCOTTISH COMPOSERS

A Night at the Chinese Opera (1987), the first opera by Scotland's Judith Weir (*b.* 1954), proved to be outstandingly inventive. Two more operas followed — *The Vanishing Bridegroom* (1990), based on a Scottish folk tale, and *Blond Eckbert* (1994), adapted from a 19th-century German short story. In 2000, Weir completed the large-scale orchestral song cycle *woman.life.song* for soprano Jessye Norman. Scottish composer James MacMillan (*b.* 1959) made his name with two impressive works: *The Confession of Isobel Gowdie* (1990), for orchestra, and *Veni, Veni, Emmanuel* (1993), for solo percussion and orchestra.

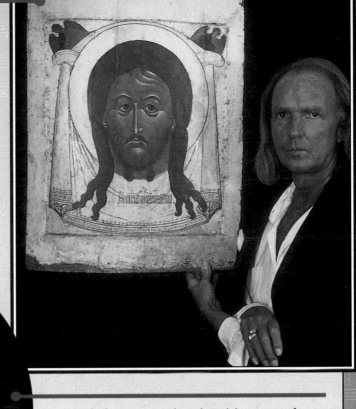

For Tavener, a Byzantine Church icon symbolizes what he tries to achieve in his music — the total absence of a composer's personal pride, in favor of a direct connection with ultimate religious truth.

Judith Weir's Blond Eckbert *explores themes of separation and mistaken identity. It was staged by the English National Opera in 1994.*

MEMORIAL

The funeral service for Diana, Princess of Wales, in 1997, brought two pieces of music resounding success. The choral *Song for Athene* (1993) made its composer, John Tavener, world famous. Elton John (*b.* 1947) performed a specially adapted version of his song "Candle in the Wind." Within a few weeks it had sold 33 million copies and topped record charts in 22 countries.

Princess Diana (center) *was a loyal patron of the London City Ballet.*

MUSIC AFTER COMMUNISM

The collapse of communism in eastern Europe meant that, at last, composers could write music without risking government disapproval. Their music often reflected the existing conditions of widespread economic and social chaos, as well as the bleak memories of the past.

Pärt has said, "I could compare my music to white light which contains all colors. Only a prism can divide the colors…this prism could be the spirit of the listener."

Giya Kancheli's large musical output includes six symphonies. He describes his task as a composer as "filling spaces that have been deserted."

A VOICE FROM ESTONIA

By the early 1980s, Estonia's Arvo Pärt (*b.* 1935), like John Tavener, had developed a style drawn partly from Eastern Orthodox chant. Pärt's *Cantus in memoriam Benjamin Britten* (1980), for strings and a single, tolling bell, was followed by other successes, including *St. John Passion* (1982), for soloists, choir, and instruments, and the liturgical *Kanon Pokajanen* (1997), for an unaccompanied choir. Pärt's music often appears on the ECM record label, which is a major force in modern music.

A TRAGIC HERITAGE

Also much recorded on the ECM label, Giya Kancheli (*b.* 1935) is a composer from the Republic of Georgia, which is on the southern border of Russia. Kancheli's style is rooted in Georgian folk music, with its lyrical sadness that is often presented within a bleak and spacious orchestral landscape, as in *Mourned by the Wind* (1989), for viola and orchestra, and *Abii ne viderem*, or *I turned away so as not to see*, (1994), for viola and strings. Russian composer Alfred Schnittke (1934–1998), responding to the repressive absurdity of Communist society, drew together extremes of different musical styles. His Fourth Symphony (1984) and his Eighth Symphony (1994) are two major examples.

LYRICAL GIFT

Elena Firsova (*b.* 1950) has a quiet and lyrical style. She is probably the most gifted Russian composer since Dmitri Shostakovich (1906–1975). In two of her finest works, *Earthly Life* (1986) and *Before the Thunderstorm* (1994), Firsova sets to music words by Russian poet Osip Mandelstam.

Elena Firsova now lives and works in England.

Schnittke's response to the hostile political world around him was nonstop composing. He produced nine symphonies, fourteen concertos, and four operas, including Life with an Idiot *(1992) and* Gesualdo *(1995).*

Schnittke's opera Dreyfus — J'Accuse *(1994) is about a French officer named Dreyfus who was unjustly convicted of treason.* J'Accuse *is a pamphlet defending Dreyfus, written by Emile Zola.*

COMPRESSED STRENGTH

The music of Hungarian composer György Kurtág (*b.* 1926) builds impressively large structures out of small vocal and instrumental forces. Kurtág's *Messages of the Late Miss R. V. Troussova* (1980) is a major song cycle for soprano and ensemble, while his *Kafka Fragments* (1986) is an hour-long work written for just a soprano voice and a solo violinist.

29

· TIME LINE ·

	WORLD EVENTS	MUSICAL EVENTS	THE ARTS	FAMOUS MUSICIANS	MUSICAL WORKS
1980	•*Start of Iran-Iraq war* •*Poland: Solidarity*	•*First Castle Donington rock festival in England*	•*Salle:* Daemonization •*Schnabel:* Jump	•*Death of former Beatle John Lennon*	•*John Adams:* Harmonium
1981	•*Egypt: President Sadat assassinated*	•*The Rolling Stones U.S. Tattoo You tour*	•*Steven Spielberg: Raiders of the Lost Ark*	•*Death of songwriter Hoagy Carmichael*	•*The Police:* Ghost in the Machine
1982	•*Falklands War: Britain defeats Argentina*	•*Michael Jackson's Thriller tops the charts*	•*Alice Walker: The Color Purple*	•*Robert Plant releases first solo album*	•*McCartney and Wonder: "Ebony and Ivory"*
1983	•*U.S. and Caribbean troops invade Grenada*	•*The Police worldwide Synchronicity tour*	•*Merce Cunningham: Quartets dancepieces*	•*Roger Waters leaves Pink Floyd*	•*Steve Reich:* The Desert Music
1984	•*India: Prime Minister Indira Gandhi killed*	•*Premiere of Tippett's The Mask of Time*	•*David Lean: A Passage to India*	•*Deaths of Marvin Gaye and Count Basie*	•*Bruce Springsteen:* Born in the USA
1985	•*USSR: Perestroika* •*Ethiopia: famine*	•*Live Aid concert in UK and Philadelphia*	•*Death of Russian-French painter Marc Chagall*	•*Death of Ricky Nelson*	•*Sting:* The Dream of the Blue Turtles
1986	•*USSR: Chernobyl nuclear disaster*	•*Exiled pianist Vladimir Horowitz plays in USSR*	•*Phantom of the Opera opens in London*	•*Paul Simon wins Grammy for Graceland*	•*Messiaen:* Livre du Saint Sacrement
1987	•*Black Monday stock market crash*	•*Madonna's first tour of UK*	•*Tom Wolfe: The Bonfire of the Vanities*	•*Death of jazz drummer Buddy Rich*	•*George Michael:* Faith •*U2:* The Joshua Tree
1988	•*End of Iran-Iraq war* •*Lockerbie air disaster*	•*Nelson Mandela's 70th birthday party concert*	•*Who Framed Roger Rabbit?*	•*Madonna stars in Speed the Plow on Broadway*	•*Van Halen:* OU812 •*Turnage:* Greek
1989	•*China: Tiananmen Square massacre*	•*20th anniversary of The Who's Tommy*	•*Amy Tan: The Joy Luck Club*	•*The Rolling Stones first tour since 1981*	•*Madonna: Like A Prayer*
1990	•*Gulf War breaks out as Iraq invades Kuwait*	•*First "Three Tenors" concert in Rome*	•*Kevin Costner stars in Dances with Wolves*	•*Deaths of Luigi Nono and Leonard Bernstein*	•*Prince:* Graffitti Bridge
1991	•*Breakup of USSR* •*Yugoslavia: civil war*	•*First Lollapalooza package tour*	•*Bulatov:* Farewell Lenin •*Quinn:* Self	•*Prince forms the New Power Generation*	•*Sondheim:* Into the Woods
1992	•*U.S.: race riots in Los Angeles*	•*Freddie Mercury "AIDS Awareness" concert*	•*Koons:* Puppy	•*Death of Olivier Messiaen*	•*Messiaen:* Eclairs sur l'au-delà
1993	•*PLO and Israel sign peace agreement*	•*Andrew Lloyd Webber's Sunset Boulevard opens*	•*Steven Spielberg: Schindler's List*	•*Gallagher brothers form Oasis*	•*Andrew Lloyd Webber:* Sunset Boulevard
1994	•*South Africa: Mandela is first black president*	•*Second "Three Tenors" concert in Los Angeles*	•*Tarantino:* Pulp Fiction	•*Death of Nirvana's Kurt Cobain*	•*Judith Weir:* Blond Eckbert
1995	•*U.S.: terrorist bomb blast in Oklahoma City*	•*Premiere of John Tavener's Apocalypse*	•*Irish poet Seamus Heaney wins Nobel Prize*	•*Death of Grateful Dead leader Jerry Garcia*	•*Oasis:* (What's the Story) Morning Glory?
1996	•*Yugoslav states sign peace treaties*	•*The Sex Pistols reform for Filthy Lucre tour*	•*Death of British artist Helen Chadwick*	•*Ry Cooder organizes Buena Vista Social Club*	•*Elliott Carter:* Symphonia
1997	•*UK: Blair named prime minister*	•*Sarah McLachlan founds Lilith Fair*	•*Rowling: Harry Potter and the Sorcerer's Stone*	•*Death of rapper Notorious B.I.G.*	•*Hans Werner Henze:* Ninth Symphony
1998	•*Birth of the euro currency*	•*Buena Vista Social Club performs in U.S.*	•*Ted Hughes: Birthday Letters*	•*Deaths of Michael Tippett and Alfred Schnittke*	•*Stockhausen:* Mittwoch aus Licht
1999	•*NATO air strikes on Yugoslavia*	•*Premiere of Berio's Cronaca del Luogo*	•*Millennium Dome built in London*	•*Death of R&B legend Curtis Mayfield*	•*Santana:* Supernatural •*Will Smith:* Willenium

GLOSSARY

avant-garde: relating to innovative works that challenge the boundaries of conventional arts.

cantata: a musical work composed for a chorus.

chamber music: instrumental music written for a small group of musicians, intended to be performed in a room or small concert hall.

conducting: directing the performance of an orchestra or a chorus, usually by waving a baton and making hand motions.

flugelhorn: a brass instrument with the sound of a bugle but looks like and has the keys of a trumpet or a cornet.

frescolike: resembling paintings made on plaster walls that often depict a story in a series of pictures.

minimalism: an artistic style or movement that promotes art or music that is spare and simple.

modernism: an artistic philosophy and practice that seeks to break with traditions of the past and find new forms of expression.

oratorio: a musical work for solo voices, chorus, and orchestra, usually with a religious theme.

panpipes: wind instruments made of short pipes, in graduated lengths, attached vertically so the mouthpieces are lined up straight across the top.

song cycle: a group of songs that are written to form a single work that often tells a story.

string quartet: a musical work for four stringed instruments, usually two violins, a viola, and a cello.

symphony: a long and usually complex musical composition for an orchestra, traditionally divided into four movements, but could have several more movements or only one movement, and may include solo or choral voices.

MORE BOOKS TO READ

Beastie Boys. In Their Own Words (series). Michael Heatley (Music Sales Corp.)

Garth Brooks: Chart-Bustin' Country. Paul Howey (Lerner)

Live Aid. Cornerstones of Freedom (series). Susan Maloney Clinton (Children's Press)

Madonna. Pop Culture Legends (series). Nicole Claro (Chelsea House)

Michael Jackson: Entertainer. Lois Nicholson (Econo-Clad Books)

Miles Davis. Black Americans of Achievement (series). Ron Frankl (Chelsea House)

One Nation Under a Groove: Rap Music and Its Roots. James Haskins (Jump at the Sun)

Tupac Shakur. They Died Too Young (series). Heather Forkos (Chelsea House)

Will Smith. Celebrity Bios (series). Kristin McCracken (Children's Press)

Wynton Marsalis: Trumpet Genius. Leslie Gourse (Franklin Watts)

WEB SITES

Andrew Lloyd Webber.
www.angelfire.com/wa/alw

Hugh Masekela Biography.
www.griot.de/biomasekela.html

John Adams.
www.earbox.com

Ladysmith Black Mambazo.
www.mambazo.com

Due to the dynamic nature of the Internet, some web sites stay current longer than others. To find additional web sites, use a reliable search engine with one or more of the following keywords: *Buena Vista Social Club, Miles Davis, Philip Glass,* hip-hop, musicals, opera, *Paul Simon, Stephen Sondheim, Sting, John Tavener, U2,* and *world music.*

INDEX

32